'In *Waterbearer*, Stuart McPher[son] what it means to be a male unflinching honesty and keen i to these poems, an illumined the aftermath of trauma: the its effect on one's closest ... ... survival. Refreshing and innovative in form and language, Stuart McPherson builds "a sudden meaningfulness" again and again, bringing brilliant insight and lyrical surprise to these pages. Water Bearer is deeply thoughtful, emotionally resonant, and lingering'

— Anindita Sengupta, *Walk Like Monsters*
    (PoetryWala / Paperwall Media 2016)

Also by Stuart McPherson

Pale Mnemonic (Legitimate Snack, 2021)

Waterbearer

McPherson

In remembrance of Lindsay

ISBN: 978-1-913642-76-1

Cover designed by Aaron Kent

Edited and typeset by Aaron Kent

Broken Sleep Books Ltd
Rhydwen,
Talgarreg,
SA44 4HB
Wales

Contents

Waterbearer

Stuart McPherson

My Daughters Photograph

Europa, I am obsessed   with storms
And you, with orbits
around my waist

              Your face born bright
                    and me, unable to bear
                         the weight of feet

So beautifully soft blue
    My gravity hasn't failed you yet

                         young moon

But maybe the size of space, my
        absorption, my propensity for vastness
                    The way that I live out here

Did you see me, Europa?
        Through a telescope or the touch of gravity
                    pushing in our lives?

Born free
And here I am, hoping for revival
                    That fear won't pull you in

That in absence you might forgive
This process of creation
This mad old way   I seem to spin

Waterbearer

My mother the comet is
ellipsing

Her reactions to fusion twist a
manic arc

Her peacock eyes weep like
false ocelli melting in the Sun

The son: the sum of stars
one to sixteen

Sitting

Not west or south
or east

As we close the doors of night
her swathing tails are everything

        (Like parenthesis)

           We are pieces of her
              waiting to be aligned

                or bravely redeemed
                    at least

Dysfunctional Family

It starts with ignition

Like when two people fuck

Hot air and gas and dust   a lust like Greek mythology
The luck of small moons
born into vastness
A feat of astrology   will you be Jupiter or Mars?

The effect of a swung fist on a tilted planet
This wreckage of asteroids crashing the surface of a
family
Wilting in a child's eyes   the shift of GN-z11 so
far away and frayed as the edges of heaven

Anti-matter
The selfishness of Sagittarius: the centre / the centaur
Why adults can't agree
An immaturity of celestial beings *so
obsessed* with their own mass

The stark violence of a star falling in on itself
We accelerate collapse
Our family photos framed

like relative theories
The abject pain of time and space
Its absent love
and inequality
The way we interpret radio signals
no one

looked after me

Portrait of a Mother

A boy left in the glow
She lay with a man
Door open, covered
with a sheet

They bathed together
He played downstairs
The television was
cruel to him

"Get me a knife" she
said
Such sharp intention
He sharpened himself

Her willowed arms
Blushed cheeks
Reddened teeth
It left from his mouth

He called downstairs
to damp skin
and cramped
like a rose

A room without air
Without eyes
On hands and knees
She coloured him in

All that flesh
Lingerie, breasts
Pursed lips
Hers to own and his

Her swollen eye
Crab shelled
A soaking bed
The purple of night

Everyone knew it
The door knew it
No feet on the mat
No knuckles to knock

She hasn't been seen
for years
An absent magicians
invisible cloak

Cassiopeia

Narcissus / you grow in me / yellowing my love
beneath a cage of ribs / a crepe paper dress / hides
your perianths / your truth

I ask you about cannibalism / your stem / your stamen
the taste of it / the way nature eats it's young
sometimes / sometimes, the way nature is disgusted

Narcissus / you sit in Poseidon's chair / so poised / *child*
so petulant / this family tree / like a mirror / petrified
like rocks / these roots / and me

Where is memory / or care / tell me about your
horticulture / your past pollination as the fate of bees

Or are you just a stung face / happy to pick off my petals
as final butterflies / fold themselves over / my constant
apologies / hung on too late

Portrait of a Stepfather

A Trojan horse
Unannounced, unpacks
He brought a black dog
The dog was black, his car was
Out back, my father's old bike

His body was bowed
White fat, a sunken chest
Washed in with the tide
Swept mermaid's purse

Boar bearded: a blackened laugh
Iridescence eclipsed
A black mouth slackened
A translucent strip
Oily purse burst; split open

I climbed on his knee
Stuck pig, stuck night
Hands on my young back
scratched lightly // no light at all
Stoop the hollow day // stop night

"She won't mind"
"She won't mind you looking in"
(Hymn) "slowly for him"
Stop night // stoop the hollow day
(Him as the Cuckoo) "come, take flight"

Fifth from The Sun / Slow Orbit

Juh uh pu ih teh urrr
Joopitturr

Juubiter   *"you've got it"*

"Dadda, can we play?"

"Just two minutes"
                                    "I'm so far away from you"

"What *is* that Dadda,
on your skin?"

"It's very red,
can I squeeze it?
                              "Don't touch it Europa, please"

"I can still see you, Dadda"
                              "thick atmosphere, not thin"

"I'll count to ten, then I'll begin to
look again, OK?"

"My book says you're a gas giant,
are you Dadda?"

"Dadda are you bright like Venus?"

                              Between us, is space

"OK Dadda, are you ready?"

"Thirty-three….thirty-four"

"No, not under the bed, not on the floor"

"Where is he?"…

"Dadda you're not being kind"

"He *must* be near"

"Not in my room, not behind the door"

"It's my turn now, Daddy, ok?"

Jupiter says,

"Daughter, I'm three and half days away from seeing your face

My wrist is tethered to this fear

How can I let you find me

Little Europa

My little moon

If I am never here"

Pornographic Material

My sex has been top shelved   with falsehoods, with farrago
Raspberried thighs cooling in the slick   of wet tape tongues

Of digitized libido   Soured compressions   Saturated
and held under   To be worn out, obsolete   A mechanistic
nodding away   all benchmarks and neatness

These emotionally   distant   formalities

Undress // Cunnilingus // Blowjob

    Missionary // Doggy // Anal // Cum

Definitions of intimacy the well-thumbed colours of a
magazine   shoved   in the trap-doored meat of my inertness

My undone sexuality falling to the floor   The disintegration
of staple crusts   dried   crumb-like

Torn tights slipped from the gloss   shoved into corners
for the dust to ask

What is masculinity, Gemini?   What is lust

What is certainty   What then   is lost

My Middle Name Is James

In the tint,
he is reflected
Under eyelids, his chalazion

My face the two acres where
we slaughtered the sheep now
dreaming in a crude pit

Our words on the pile
The thud of a blunt axe
A consonant, a vowel

Damp cork
My forehead a stiff
leather cloth

I hold his violence in a pan with
the chipped teeth of a pig
Some *economic cuts*

I miss him sometimes
but my father
is dead

And unavailable to explain
why he is hiding
in my body

Preservative

The village could steal his voice he found, observing where they hoisted up the warm vessel that his old man had used to float in.

"You're hard to talk to" she said, never looking inside his mouth.

Or knowing that when it got snatched, that it bobbed quietly in the Adder jar, its formaldehyde suspended on a window-sill just two minutes flight from where she always slept.

We knocked the serpent dead, and they all knew what was born from the northern sky

His voice slid back, *non-venomous,* but she wasn't there, and still didn't manage to ask the right questions.

My Brother is Lost

My brother is
summer clothes
Boat shoes and shorts
packed in a case

He climbed inside
and sent himself away
Neatly folded
You'll see him still,
in the east

In his throat you'll
find a crag of
pink tourmaline,
unswallowed

If you felt his skin
he would be feathered
like a Jay

He can be heard
vibrating gently
Familiar frequencies
in the ageing of
his face

Sarcophagus

Sister, he filled you full of leaves   *This is not how you left*
but how you would leave

I knew you'd have to go   little dandelion

Little dandelion   in your little sarcophagus
Hospital hemmed blue, so full of empty bottles,   and *you*

You'd given up your twilight years   The gulps of a muddy
stream had taken them   to dream of estuaries in lieu

Of cruel things, cruel birds.   No one else would have cooed
but you

Sister, my pockets are full of guilt, I left you   *You never left me*
guilt

You were picked by a mother's hand,   snapped at the stem

Set down in water   lapping at the leaking milk

That washed us away from land
That washed   me   away   from   you

And the milk on my fingers   hung out to dry
with the guilt of a spider   hanging its silk

The sarcophagus held you little dandelion, held you on its cushion

My hip bone spoke to the floor   Had purple
conversations for three nights   doors swinging for your life
as they came in   and out

In the pulpit my judgement   on my lips my judgement
Near as I whispered   Confessed all to your

open ear   so maybe they would hear   the words falling
floating through the frame   *Forgive Me*

And you,   so small in your little Viking boat would always
give more   If only you could hear   *Please live, do you*
hear?

Sister,   the leaves are in your blood and now your lungs are trees

My hand on your head   The wind disappeared from the
window It had lingered by your husband   by your bed

I kept looking to the empty street below   so cold
The years paused   passed through the cracks in my fingers

En-route to take your place in the sky   you rose up little
dandelion   little pharaoh   *Goodbye*

You are Egyptian now sister   *You are in the leaves*
The trees hold you   *Take your leave*

The nurses left   The family in the dark had
gone   Alarms still spoke

The park across the way was still   Planes
stalled   Buses
stopped

We bulged, ballooned, shrank in our shoes   Paused the rain
Ate silence revealed in clouds   carving hieroglyphics into
the crowns of ornate building tops   (Your name)

You're free little dandelion   *You burned brighter than me*

You appear from time-to-time   Christmas letters   a blanket
set   a sting like lime   squeezed on a tongue

I'd never reply but if time were south,   I'd travel
Be better   Maybe pick up the phone

Migrate to a place of care and love   and not this empty space

This regret   This   dull   bare   stone

You were so young little dandelion   but not alone
Sleeping in your little sarcophagus   where you fell

                                                    (I'm sorry)

Self Portrait

A twilight machinery

The reprise of the sea beneath   an anchored ship
This non-empathy of   hurt
A nothingness   when someone you vaguely know
dies

Unnecessary trips

Every side of every building ever built
and the gap   gap   gaps   between guilt

The horsehead nebula   reflected

Sat on slats
The length of a bed seen through dust / misdirected

Wind in a valley playing dead

Dismemberment of thin snow
Wood knots   Amber Sap

Every Morning There Are Two of Me

I climb into bed, this long flat knife
The way a surgeon re-opens a slow wound

There are twice the loosening lights
Alpha Aquarii netted in the orange of a bowing lamp

Outside we are ready to be thrown into the long trees
As the street holds the hollow sound of rope

The morning questions a casket lottery

The lies of our rested shapes shepherd away paleness,
like a crook

Why I'm Terrible at Goodbyes

The bodies of fireworks sick with gunpowder, hold sadness like the skeleton of a match.

Dead, they are fireworks and left. The end of things or every end of everything or nothing whatsoever.

Fireworks are bodies left of sound but not light. Held in the damp tube with my thumb impressed, I see your face as we said goodbye.

Fireworks left there are dead for me to throw away and the gardens are quiet.

No one cares to sit in Cassiopeia's chair. They are closed. They always are. The fireworks are empty and strewn.

And I am left.

Perfectionism

The marble rolls to me
                                    when I work
Or aspirate the possibility of futures

or build
                                    a sudden meaningfulness
And its twelve edges
investigate the thinness of my skin

                                    sharp as the failure of citrus
No blood but dust; like a flour bag
puffing out.

I file it, bathe it in acid, cast it under
the north star to

                                    amnesiate

But it remembers and rolls to my
feet with its knocking squareness

                                    I hide it
from my daughter
                                    in the deep clay outside
but still it comes right back

unchanged

Beginnings of Hypervigilance

Like the Northern Lights knife nicked
Stretched plastic or a syncopated heart

Something asunder, a quickening away
of life, the beat of a non-drum, a non -

Rhododendron. Its lack of optimism at
a windowpane tap tap tapping pink &

ill-explained. A white retracted cats claw
Checking hourly, that dry place for rain

Self-Help Manual Written in Invisible Ink

And then   as if revolving around the sun   he started to spin
Language a lie   spun by two separate lives
One before   one after   *He had made it this far*

They kept talking to him about nature   its benefits
He thought about a leaf   blown onto the shelf of a high rock
into seams with all the others never quite seen or   felt
between fingers   and rubbed   into dust

His lungs now thin   and unable to accommodate this
present air   or past   the golden hands of sunlight existing
solely to burn skin   How do you meditate when all you do
is sit lotus legged and see the Ohm as   *just sound released*

These *must- have* strategies   Some preparation for
transcendence   his previous dependence on horoscopes and
zodiacs   His worldly place   in the hands of fate
The chime of Tingsha   no line   no trajectory between what is

or has been   and definitions of identity   all down to
conjunction   Excuses for defunct people
Benign fun / benign body   *What is running but*
the taste of blood on your tongue?   Or a heaving in and out

Some need for self-care   a test   and before she
left   she talked about the way he ignored himself
Something held within   The knowingness of
a peak worn down   beneath water   beneath wind

Engineering Self-Worth

How can a mirror know itself
like a door knows itself
with its letting in and out
Or that sense of self felt in
the growing bones

//

A cracked mirror is du
                    pli
                    cation

Its judgement silver backed
The veneer of my mother's earrings
My father's confinement to his shadow chair
A knife swung like a kite to
                              stab
                              the
                              earth

The time to become *something*
Or   mis   align
                                        ment
His droning voice is   mine
An understanding of sketches
                                    my outline
A scribbling like trees scratched on paper

Abstractly

Unfair to mirrors
                maybe
But they infer the scratch of   self
                                            freely
undone

Like Mars screams war
                              but isn't
'On killing'
                an unloaded gun
                                          (retorts)

//

There are no answers
                    in mirrors
                              They do not know to
look up
          Or the crow (night)   fled

  Or what it is to be un-buried and *Orienteer*
                          'explore fear' lead instead

                                        True North

//

I   will
                not

                          bow
                                                to

                you

                                        (night)

Something Had to Die So That I Could Live

In the beginning of
beautiful death,
There were no signs

In fading light
pulled out the twins
One white, one still

Motherly clicks
The wetness of hay
Her bleating eyes

Looking, then licked
Swung twice and
slapped

The man wrapping
Aries in a sheet,
took away the old

By the daffodils
set him down
Whilst the new

Danced in the grass
Like snow
for the beautiful dead

Aquarius looking for Leo

When you meet him
　　　　you can undress,
　　　　Join up the asterisms
　　　　with your
　　　　　　　　nakedness

Unpick the seams
　　　　running groin to chest
　　　　Let Mars fall out
　　　　like a heart
　　　　The rest fall out as
　　　　pomegranates
　　　　　　　　ageing redness

There will be a time
　　　　to repurpose
　　　　For beauty
　　　　To fill yourself with the
　　　　teeth of a snake
　　　　To cultivate birches
　　　　　　　　Absorb aquila

Bearer,　　there can
　　　　be water
　　　　when you have found
　　　　what can be
　　　　poured from you

　　　　　　　　Aquarius

Acknowledgments

Perfectionism first appeared in 'After the Pause' March 2021

Cassiopeia & *Engineering Self-Worth* first appeared in 'Selcouth Station' February 2021

Thanks also to the following poets for their support, and inspiration; Aaron Kent, Serge Neptune, Zoë Brigley, Anindita Sengupta, Tom Snarsky, Naush Sabah, Colin Bancroft, Briony Hughes & Osmosis Press, Michelle Maloney King & Beir Bua Journal, Anna Saunders, Louise Mather, JP Seabright & Leia Butler at Full House Literary Magazine, P.A Morbid & The Black Light Engine Room Press, and Kathleen Gresham Everett.

Thank you to my wife Caroline, my daughter Dorrie and my sister Amanda

This book is dedicated to the survivors

LAY OUT YOUR UNREST